HYPOTHETICALLY

40 Writing Prompts
A Workbook
For Storytellers
Vol 1

By Aubrey Bjork

ISBN 978-1-965067-12-3

Start writing, no matter what.
The water does not flow until the faucet is turned on.

LOUIS L'AMOUR

1

You've been sent to spend the night in a haunted house. What's one thing you take with you?

You've been cursed by a djinn to play one sport for the rest of your life. Which one is it? **2**

3 Your car has been zapped with a bolt of magical lightning. What happens now?

_____

_____

_____

_____

_____

_____

_____

_____

_____

_____

_____

_____

_____

_____

You're about to open your bake shop for the very first time. What's foremost on your mind?

4

5

A winged messenger arrives on your doorstep. You open the letter and read—

You pass an abandoned animal on the street. **6**
What kind of animal is it? What do you do?

_____

_____

_____

_____

_____

_____

_____

_____

_____

_____

_____

_____

_____

7

A friend of yours walks pass a bathroom mirror, screams, and passes out. What happens next?

_____

_____

_____

_____

_____

_____

_____

_____

_____

_____

_____

_____

_____

_____

_____

You notice a strange rock on the sidewalk. It reads, "for the one who craves wisdom." What do you do ?

8

9

You're about to prepare the most important three-course meal of your life. Who is it for and what are you cooking?

Riding on the bus one day, it suddenly takes off and soars into the sky. What happens next? **10**

11

You're trying to choose a movie to watch one evening and notice that all of the titles say the same thing—

You've one the local mayor for a day competition.
What's your first act in office? **12**

13

The watch on your wrist ticks slowly. Your time is almost up. What's about to happen?

_____

_____

_____

_____

_____

_____

_____

_____

_____

_____

_____

_____

_____

_____

_____

_____

_____

_____

You can grant one animal the power to speak.
Which animal do you choose and what does it say? **14**

15

You are in charge of creating a new holiday. When is it and what do you celebrate?

Your car breaks down in the middle of nowhere. What do you do next? **16**

17

Sometime past midnight, there's a scratching under your bedroom door. You look down and see—

_____

_____

_____

_____

_____

_____

_____

_____

_____

_____

_____

_____

_____

_____

_____

_____

_____

You're headed out the door for the best vacation of your entire life. Suddenly—

18

19

You're a songwriter for a famous group.
What's the name of the next big hit?

Early one morning, a little bird perches on your window. It opens its beak and—

20

21

You spin the wheel of magical consequences. What do you hope it doesn't land on?

There's something missing from your pocket— **22**
something very important. It's—

23

You go to sleep and wake up the next morning, 10 years later. What's the first thing you see?

You have mastery over one element. Which one is it and what do you do? **24**

25

You've finally done it. You officially own the world's largest collection of—

You've received an envelope with gold lettering in the mail. You open it, and it reads— **26**

_____

_____

_____

_____

_____

_____

_____

_____

_____

_____

_____

_____

_____

_____

27

You're foiled again, trapped by the ineffable powers of—

You eat half of your breakfast cereal before you look down into the bowl and realize— **28**

29

Write an acceptance speech for an award you didn't win.

Of all the things that could have
happened that Friday morning, you
didn't think it would be that...

30

31

You're an inventor and you've just had a breakthrough. You're just one step away from—

You've decided to open your own
detective agency. For your very first
case, you investigate—

32

33

The wizard at the store has given you a magical gumball. When you chew it, you'll be able to—

_____

_____

_____

_____

_____

_____

_____

_____

_____

_____

_____

_____

_____

_____

_____

_____

That last person you ever expected to knock on your door just did. And they brought— **34**

35

You've been sent to film the most important event on your continent. It's—

You've designed the perfect chair, and your local furniture store has asked you about it. You say—

36

37

The cashier at the grocery store looks at your I.D. and says, "Oh my word, you're—"

Typing an email one day, your computer types back. "Where did you put—"

39

You have been granted the ability to master one skill. What skill is it and why?

The last thing you remembered, you were crossing the bridge on the way to an appointment. Now—

ABOUT THE AUTHOR

Aubrey Bjork loves her family, fairy tale retellings, and warm mugs of hot chocolate, preferably fresh from the Keurig.

In her spare time, she writes books like these, audtions for community theater productions, and watches Godzilla movies, including the horrible ones from the 60s.

Her work has appeared in *Foliate Oak Literary Magazine, The Columbia Missourian,* and *Balloons,* a literary magazine for children.

She's haunted nightly by some of the prompts in this book and hopes you appreciate them.

www.ingramcontent.com/pod-product-compliance
Lightning Source LLC
Chambersburg PA
CBHW081539120626
46550CB00009B/2796